BELLEVILLE

BOOKS BY AMY HERZOG
PUBLISHED BY TCG

Belleville

4000 Miles and *After the Revolution*

The Great God Pan

BELLEVILLE

Amy Herzog

THEATRE COMMUNICATIONS GROUP
NEW YORK
2014

Belleville is published by Theatre Communications Group, Inc.,
520 8th Avenue, 24th Floor, New York, NY 10018-4156

The publication of *Belleville*, by Amy Herzog, through TCG's Book Program, is made possible in part by the New York State Council on the Arts with the support of Governor Andrew Cuomo and the New York State Legislature.

Special thanks to Paula Marie Black for her generous support of this publication.

TCG books are exclusively distributed to the book trade by Consortium Book Sales and Distribution.

LIBRARY OF CONGRESS CATALOGING-IN-PUBLICATION DATA
Herzog, Amy.
Belleville / Amy Herzog.—First edition.
pages cm
ISBN 978-1-55936-457-7 (paperback)
ISBN 978-1-55936-771-4 (ebook)
I. Title.
PS3608.E79B45   2014
812'.6—dc23   2014027910

Book design and composition by Lisa Govan
Cover design by Carol Devine Carson

First Edition, October 2014
Third printing, June 2020

Acknowledgments

I would like to thank James Bundy, Jennifer Kiger and Amy Boratko of the Yale Repertory Theatre for their infinite patience; and Virgil Blanc for his indispensable help with the colloquial French.

BELLEVILLE

Belleville was commissioned by and received its world premiere at the Yale Repertory Theatre (James Bundy, Artistic Director; Victoria Nolan, Managing Director) in New Haven, Connecticut, on October 27, 2011. It was directed by Anne Kauffman; the set design was by Julia C. Lee, the costume design was by Mark Nagle, the lighting design was by Nina Hyun Seung Lee and the sound design was by Robert Kaplowitz. The production stage manager was Gina Noele Odierno. The cast was:

ABBY	Maria Dizzia
ZACK	Greg Keller
ALIOUNE	Gilbert Owuor
AMINA	Pascale Armand

This production of *Belleville* transferred to New York Theatre Workshop (James C. Nicola, Artistic Director; William Russo, Managing Director) in New York City on March 3, 2013. The cast and personnel remained the same with the following exceptions: the lighting design was by Ben Stanton, the production stage manager was Terri K. Kohler and Alioune was played by Phillip James Brannon.

Scene One

The main room of an apartment in Belleville. An old building with character; many layers of paint cover the original moldings. Tastefully but inexpensively decorated. A mix of convincing knockoffs of stylish modern furniture pieces and accents that suggest North African fabrics and crafts. IKEA meets Parisian flea market. Floor pillows augment the scant seating options. The residents here are temporary.

At lights up, it's late afternoon. No lights are on in the apartment. Indirect sunlight filters in from a window or two.

From within the bedroom, we can barely hear music.

A key in the lock.

The front door opens and Abby enters in lots of winter layers, carrying a yoga mat and several shopping bags. She drops the mat, the bags and her winter coat on the floor. She closes the door. She turns on a light. She goes to the couch and drapes herself over it, her back in a deep arch. She closes her eyes.

In her stillness, she hears the beat of nearby music and indistinct voices. She opens her eyes and listens. She stands. She walks slowly and quietly to the bedroom door, where she stops and listens. Hesitantly, she turns the knob and opens the door. She screams. She runs to the front door.

With the door open, we can identify the music as a porn soundtrack. Zack enters from the bedroom, buttoning his jeans.

ZACK: Hi.
ABBY: Hey.
ZACK: I thought you had class.
ABBY: No one showed.

(Brief pause.)

ZACK: Probably people have already left town.
ABBY: Yeah, maybe.

(Pause.)

ABBY *(Simultaneously)*: What are you doing home?
ZACK *(Simultaneously)*: So you went shopping?
ABBY: What?
ZACK: You went shopping?

(Brief pause.)

ABBY: Just for the last few Christmas presents. I want to mail everything by tomorrow to be safe.
ZACK: Did you use the new credit card?
ABBY: Yup. It works.
ZACK: Good! What did you get?
ABBY: For your parents some, um. Tea.
ZACK: That's fine, they'll like it.
ABBY: Well.
ZACK: They'll pretend to, which is the same thing with them.
ABBY: And chocolate for my dad from that place he remembers going once with my mom. And for the baby, this Eiffel tower, um. Onesie.

(She shows him.)

ZACK: Cute.

ABBY *(Apologetically)*: My sister will like it.

ZACK: Maybe the child will be born with a keen sense of irony.
Maybe she'll wear the onesie ironically.

ABBY: Not if she takes after / her father.

ZACK: Her father, true.
That's it?

ABBY: Zack, what are you—?

ZACK: What?

ABBY: Doing home?

(Pause.)

ZACK: I took the afternoon off.

ABBY: Why didn't you call me?

ZACK: Because I thought you were teaching.

ABBY: Are you *sick*, or—?

(Brief pause; he misunderstands.)

ZACK: I'm sorry, meaning—?

ABBY: I mean are you—do you have a / cold—?

ZACK: Just . . . kinda tired. Playing hooky. I know.

(He slaps himself on the wrist.)

You don't look so good.

ABBY: I just . . . need a sec . . .

ZACK: This is such a big deal?

ABBY: I guess not.

ZACK: I mean, it's embarrassing, for me.

ABBY: I don't mean for you to be embarrassed.

ZACK: No? Because you're having a *slightly* Victorian reaction.

ABBY: I am?

ZACK: Mmmm—

ABBY: I thought I was home alone. It was a little scary.
ZACK: Just me.

(He smiles. She smiles back, making an effort.)

I'm gonna jump in the shower, if that's cool.
ABBY: Yup!

(He hesitates.)

I'm fine! I am cool, this is me being cool. Go. Finish up.
    (Off his look) Kidding! Maybe, or maybe making a real
suggesti— Go. I'm not talking, go.

(He exits into the bathroom. She is still. The shower starts
offstage. She opens her eyes. She goes toward the bedroom.
She hesitates at the threshold, then goes in. From the bedroom,
offstage, we hear the sound of the porn soundtrack resume. It
plays for a few seconds, then stops. Abby reenters from the
bedroom, stony. She closes the door behind her.
    A knock at the door jolts Abby back into alertness. She goes
to the door and opens it to reveal Alioune.)

Hey.
ALIOUNE: Abby!
ABBY: What's up?
ALIOUNE: Sorry, I—
ABBY: What?
ALIOUNE: I thought I saw Zack come in a little while ago.
ABBY: Yeah, he's in the shower.
ALIOUNE: I'll come later.
ABBY: It's okay, come in.

(Abby walks back into the apartment, leaving the door open,
then turns to see that Alioune is hesitating.)

Come on, he'll just be a couple minutes.

ALIOUNE: You don't mind?
ABBY: Are you hungry? I made—

(*She exits. Alioune comes all the way into the apartment, uneasily. He notices a book on the coffee table and stoops to look at it. He straightens up slightly guiltily as Abby reenters with a tray of sugar cookies in Christmas cutouts.*)

ALIOUNE: Thank you.

(*He takes one, sees she is still holding the tray out, and politely takes another. She takes one herself.*)

ABBY: You can look at that, I just put it out for that reason.

(*He picks up the book and dutifully looks through it.*)

ALIOUNE: It looks nice.
ABBY: It was nice.
ALIOUNE: Big.
ABBY: A hundred and fifty people. Midsize.
ALIOUNE (*Impressed*): Is this your house?

(*Abby laughs.*)

ABBY: No, that's a manor.
ALIOUNE: A—?
ABBY: It was somebody's house once, and now it's a place you rent for weddings. We don't have a fountain at my house. Or a rose garden. Or ice sculptures, on a typical day.
ALIOUNE: It's very, it's . . .
ABBY: Yeah, it was fine, if I were gonna do it all over again I'd have like ten people meet us at city hall and spend the money traveling with Zack for a year before he started med school. But we were the first of all our friends to do it, we didn't have any basis for . . . It was nice, though, I was really happy that day.

(Alioune turns the page. Something makes him smile.)

What?

ALIOUNE: It's Zack's face, he's so—

ABBY: I know, he's such a ham. He hates having his picture taken.

(He turns the last few pages and politely replaces the book on the table.)

ALIOUNE: Thank you for showing me.

(Brief pause.)

ABBY: How's Amina?

ALIOUNE: Fine.

ABBY: And the baby?

ALIOUNE: Great.

(He gives her a thumbs up to accentuate his answer. More silence as they eat.)

Will you go home? For the holidays?

ABBY: Oh—Zack didn't tell you?

ALIOUNE: No.

ABBY: We can't. There's a problem. With the visas, I don't understand it, honestly, but apparently we won't be able to get back / in if we—

ALIOUNE: Oh, no.

ABBY: Yeah, it sucks because my sister's about to have a baby. Like any minute. So it'll be the baby's first Christmas. Not like she'll know we're not there.

ALIOUNE: Your sister?

ABBY: The baby. She. My *sister*. Will know. My sister is not happy about it. I'm not sure if Zack mentioned that my mom died a few years ago?

ALIOUNE: Yes, and I want to say, that I am / so sorry—

ABBY: No no no, just to explain, that holidays in my family have become especially *weighted*. Almost to the exclusion of fun, it's like hours of meaningful eye contact, it's exhausting, actually. But no, I'm being glib, I fucking love Christmas with my family.

ALIOUNE: I'm so sorry.

ABBY: Well.

(She shrugs: "what can you do?")

What are you guys doing for Christmas?

ALIOUNE: We're Muslim.

ABBY: Oh— *(The cookies)* Oh!

ALIOUNE: It's all right.

ABBY: I just gave you a—

ALIOUNE: It's okay, we're not very strict.

ABBY: Well I hope not, since you're in the process of eating an angel. I feel so dumb that I didn't . . . because you guys are from . . .

ALIOUNE: Amina was born here. Originally, I'm from Dakar.

ABBY: Uh-huh. Which is in—

ALIOUNE: Senegal.

ABBY: Right. Which is Muslim.

ALIOUNE: Mostly.

ABBY: Sorry.

ALIOUNE: It is really, it's okay.

ABBY: No, yeah, it's good, I'll just set out to confirm every stereotype you may have about Americans.

ALIOUNE: The French, they are not so much better.

ABBY: That's comforting. Because the superior thing that they do, it's very *convincing*. Do you know that I get nervous before grocery shopping here? I have to psych myself up for every interaction, it's deeply sad. You're very sweet but you don't have to keep eating those.

ALIOUNE: I am afraid you do not like it here.

ABBY: Me? Oh no, I love it. It's the city of love, or the city of lights, which is it? Is it both? And I especially love this neighborhood, I love the—um, well I hate the word "diversity," I just feel like a button on a denim jacket in the late eighties, oh God there's no way you get that reference, but it's so—but, you know, there's a lot of life here, I don't feel like I'm living in an artifact, and it's nice not being the only, um, foreigners, you know, feeling like we are among others making a life in this sometimes hostile . . .

(She really wishes she hadn't started talking.)

Anyway it is *not about me*. Zack is doing research to prevent *children* from contracting *AIDS*, I can be a big girl and deal with a little homesickness, right? So, what do Muslims do for Christmas?

ALIOUNE: Uh . . .

ABBY: Joke, Alioune, that was a / joke.

(A sickening thud comes from off, where the shower is running. Alioune and Abby look at each other. No other noise beyond the sound of the shower.)

Zack?

(No response.)

Homey, you okay?

(She knocks on the door, no response. She opens it.)

You okay?

(Muffled, Zack's voice off. Abby goes into the bathroom and closes the door. Alioune stands, uncomfortable. Abby reenters.)

He's fine. He just dropped the shampoo. God, I'm jumpy.

ALIOUNE: I will come back.

ABBY: He'll just be a sec, I told him you're here.

ALIOUNE: I feel it's not—I have chosen a bad time.

ABBY: No, I—it's not a bad time, I'm sorry if I've, that I'm such a downer—

ALIOUNE: No, Abigail—

ABBY: I'm like going on and on about—I really apologize, I just don't have enough to do.

ALIOUNE: Stop. Stop apologizing.

(Brief pause.)

You know, Zack, he always say you are a wonderful actress.

ABBY: Really? Yeah, I'm all right. But to be an actor you have to love to suffer and I only *like* to suffer.

I'm a yoga teacher right now. And that's fine. The dharma teaches you to say "good enough." You know?

(Pause. The shower stops. She calls off.)

Zack, our landlord urgently needs to smoke a bowl with you.

ZACK *(Offstage)*: What?

ABBY: Hurry up, you're keeping Alioune waiting!

ZACK *(Offstage)*: Oh, *pardon, une minute, / Alioune!*

ALIOUNE: *Ça va, ne t'en fais pas!*

ABBY: *Ça va.* That means "I'm okay."

ALIOUNE: Or "it's okay." I see your French classes are proceeding at a very advanced, euh / rate.

ABBY: Oh that's sarcasm, that's good. I stopped going, actually.

ALIOUNE: Why?

(Around this time Zack crosses from the bathroom to the bedroom in a towel.)

ABBY: Because the teacher made fun of my pronunciation, and because everyone speaks English here. As long as I know how to say "*pardon*" when I bump into someone and "*laissez-moi tranquille*" when men bother me on the metro / I—

ALIOUNE: A lot of men give you trouble here?

(Brief pause.)

ABBY: Surprise though that may / be—

ALIOUNE: Not a surprise.

ABBY: Too late, you gave yourself away.

ALIOUNE: I only, I am disappointed, in my other, how do you say—?

ABBY: My fellow men.

ALIOUNE: Thank you, that they do not treat you with respect.

ABBY: Uh-huh. How old do you think I am?

(He considers.)

ALIOUNE: Thirty . . . two?

ABBY: Okay, get out. Seriously, get out.

ALIOUNE: Seventeen.

ABBY: Funny. I'm twenty-eight.

ALIOUNE: Sorry, your . . . *(He gestures vaguely toward her hair)*

ABBY: We gray early in my family, okay? God, you can see it from there?

How old are you?

ALIOUNE: Twenty-five.

ABBY: *What?!*

ALIOUNE: What did you think?

ABBY: You have two kids! And a property management business!

ALIOUNE: Yes. And I am twenty-five.

ABBY: Let me ask you this. When you were little, did your parents intone, over and over, "It doesn't matter what you do when you grow up as long as you're happy?"

(Brief pause.)

ALIOUNE: No.

ABBY: I am increasingly convinced that is the worst thing you can say to a child. May I never say that to my children.

Zack!

ZACK *(Offstage)*: What?

16

ABBY: How old do you think Alioune is?

(Brief pause.)

ZACK *(Offstage)*: Twenty-four?

(Alioune laughs.)

ABBY: He told you!

ALIOUNE: I don't think so.

ABBY: He has two kids!

ZACK *(Offstage)*: Yeah, scientifically, I'm not having a problem with that timeline.

ABBY *(Quietly)*: Where oh where have my twenties gone?

(The bedroom door opens and Zack enters, dressed, wet hair, with his laptop.)

ZACK: Sorry to keep you waiting, man.

ALIOUNE: Now I understand, why are the hot water bills so high since you move in.

ABBY: Oh! Oh no, that's / me.

ZACK: That's Abby.

ABBY: I'm the worst, I take so many baths. It's a compulsion. I wake up in the morning and I'm like *I will not take a bath today*, and / then—

ZACK: She gets cold.

ABBY: I am perpetually chilled, and it's the / only thing—

ZACK: Blue fingernails, it's spooky. Once / she—

ABBY: Please don't tell this story.

ZACK: Why? Alioune / won't—

ABBY: Fine, but do the short version.

ZACK: We had a seminar together, in college, and it met in the basement of this / old—

ABBY: It was freezing!

ZACK: It was, it was unacceptable.

ABBY: Zack is never cold, and his teeth would chatter by the end.

ZACK: Oh because it was a three-hour seminar. The professor was this old phlegmatic—

ABBY: Short version.

ZACK: So this one class meeting it was below freezing outside and Abby had herself contorted into / this—

ABBY: I have to sort of wrap my limbs around each other sometimes to keep warm.

(She demonstrates.)

ALIOUNE: . . . Oh.

ZACK: And when class ended and we walked out she said her leg felt weird so she pulled up her jeans, and her left calf—

ABBY: It was my right calf.

ZACK: Her *left* calf, you're wrong, was swollen to like twice its normal size. Because the way she was sitting, she had blocked off a vein or, artery or / whatever and—

ABBY: Can you tell this man attended *medical* school?

ZACK: And, shhh, and all this blood had pooled there. It was really grotesque.

ABBY: Thanks.

ALIOUNE: That's . . .

ABBY: Yeah, it's disgusting. I went to the health center and the doctor had never seen anything like it so she sent me to the ER. But by the time they could see me it had returned to normal so I just felt like an asshole. I was like, "yeah, I don't really know what I'm doing here, my leg was swollen . . . before," and they were like, ". . . awesome, so glad we had this talk."

See, it's not a good story.

ZACK: It is, however, the story of how we got together.

ABBY: Zack stayed with me the whole time.

ZACK: Even though you were desperately in love with somebody else, and / would be for quite some time.

ABBY: Blah blah blah, can we not . . . ?

ALIOUNE: You should take as many baths as you need.

(Pause.)

ABBY: All right, I'll leave you two to your devious purpose.

(She begins to exit.)

ZACK: Hey, I was thinking in the shower, maybe we should go
on a D-A-T-E tonight.
ABBY: Ooohhh! A D-A-T-E.
ALIOUNE: Why do you spell it?
ABBY: He thinks I'm like a dog, if I get too excited I'll pee myself.
ZACK: It's been a while since we went on a D-A-T-E.
ABBY: You feeling bad about something?
ZACK: You trying to start something in front of Alioune?
ABBY: I guess you're just *assuming* I'm available.
ZACK: I should have asked. Are you available?
ABBY: I think I can switch a few things around.
ZACK: I'd like that.

(Her phone rings.)

ABBY: That'll be my father. He's already been awake for a few
hours without being reassured of his centrality in my exis-
tence. *(She picks up)* Hi Daddy. It was canceled. *(On her
way out)* Because nobody showed up. What do you call a
yoga teacher with no students? This has been your daily
Zen koan, by Abby. *(To Zack)* Window.

(She exits. Zack performs falling over in exhaustion.)

ALIOUNE: No no, she—it was fine.
ZACK: Sorry. Whatever you just had to deal with, sorry.

*(Over the following, Zack packs a bowl. He also opens his
laptop to select music, briefly typing something.)*

ALIOUNE: It was my fault. I offended her, because I thought she
was thirty-two.

ZACK: Oh no!

ALIOUNE: Actually I thought she was older, I thought thirty-two was a / safe—

ZACK: Sorry I left you stranded out here, man. She walked in on me earlier. Um. On the computer.

ALIOUNE *(Brief pause)*: Oh—oh, shit!

ZACK: Yup. Yes.

ALIOUNE: Was it—very nasty?

ZACK: The screen was turned away from her.

ALIOUNE: Good.

ZACK: But. Yes.

(They both laugh.)

She's trying to go off her medication. Not trying, she's going off. It's torture. It's torture. But I'm not allowed to say anything because that would be *unsupportive*. And this is a *period of transition*. Meanwhile I'm thinking of resorting to mashing them up in her food, it's just . . . *so* not a good idea.

ALIOUNE: She was on . . . ?

ZACK: Oh, like an antidepressant, antianxiety. She started taking it when her mom was dying, and never imagined that five years later, yadda yadda, but as far as I was concerned that shit was worth its weight in *gold*, it was . . . *(Proffering)* Green for you, friend.

(They smoke over the following.)

I'm just, I'm losing my mind, because for the last five years all she's talked about is Paris, her parents had some amazing trip to Paris in like 1970-something, she thinks Paris will be the cure for all her, whatever, so I give up a really good residency to take this job, no complaints, it's a great job, but now we're here, and she quits her French classes, and she's uncomfortable in the neighborhood—

ALIOUNE: She's uncomfortable in *Belleville*?

ZACK: She would never admit it, but . . . anyway. You see what I'm dealing with.

ALIOUNE: Sorry.

ZACK: Yeah, it's a nightmare. It's very dark in there.

(Zack does something briefly on the computer.)

How's Amina?

ALIOUNE: Fine. The kids, they're fine. Uh . . .

(Abby enters from the bedroom, still on the phone, holding Zack's ringing phone out toward him.)

ABBY *(Quietly)*: Work.

(Zack takes the phone and Abby returns to the bedroom, talking again to her dad.)

Not yet, but / we finally got to Père Lachaise. It was rainy though so we didn't . . .

ZACK: Sorry dude—one second.
      Allo? Bonjour Brigitte, ça va?
      Ouais, je me souviens. A dix heures, n'est-ce pas? Ouais.
      Non, pas du tout, merci. A demain.

(He hangs up.)

My assistant. What were we . . . ? Your kids! I saw your older one, in the / hall.

ALIOUNE: Ousmane.

ZACK: Yeah he's such a little person, he's such a little *guy*.

ALIOUNE: He is climbing stairs now, no hands, this is the new, uh . . .

ZACK: Incredible.

ALIOUNE: Yes. I want to have another, I want a girl, but Amina . . .

ZACK: She's done.

ALIOUNE: She's done. For now. We'll see.

(The jovial mood somehow drains away. Neither of them wants to have this conversation.)

So . . .

ZACK: I know. I know what you're gonna say.

ALIOUNE: Yeah. I really did not expect, after our last / talk.

ZACK: So what *happened*, I had it all in the account, this is as of forty-eight hours ago, what I didn't realize was that she had done all this Christmas shopping on the credit card, and unbeknownst to me made this like monumental *transfer*—

ALIOUNE: I'm sure there's a very good / reason—

ZACK: Which I did not discover / until this morning—

ALIOUNE: But it doesn't matter. I mean. Sorry, but I don't care. I don't care why anymore.

(Pause.)

ZACK: Oh-*kay*.

ALIOUNE: Listen, my uncle, he looked at the accounts. I . . . hadn't told him, because I knew he wouldn't allow it, and I thought you would—before he found out. But he saw, and now he is saying he can't trust me. You know, my uncle, he raised me, since I was six. A month ago he was asking me would I like to be his partner, now he is saying he can't trust me.

ZACK: Oh man, I'm so sorry—

ALIOUNE: No, it's—I'm not telling you to feel sorry for me, because it's my mistake. I don't know why I even tell you this, about my uncle.

ZACK: Because we're friends, and I feel like shit about putting you in that position, I really do.

ALIOUNE: Well that doesn't matter.

ZACK: It matters to me.

ALIOUNE: Zack, I need the money. All four months you owe me. Soon. Tomorrow, or—

ZACK: *Tomorrow?*

ALIOUNE: Okay, Friday. Or you have to go. I'm sorry, but . . .

(Pause. Zack goes to pack another bowl.)

Not for me, thanks.

ZACK: For me, buddy, for me.

ALIOUNE: You know how much respect I have for your work.

ZACK: Uh-huh.

ALIOUNE: I mean that. I told my uncle, I even asked if we could make a deal with you, because—in a way, that's like giving to a charity—

ZACK: *Thanks.*

ALIOUNE: I tried to help, all right?

ZACK: It shouldn't be a problem, I can get it by Friday.

ALIOUNE: Yes?

ZACK: Yeah dude.

ALIOUNE: Well . . . good.

(Zack tokes. He offers to Alioune, who hesitates, then accepts one more hit.)

I feel much better, that we spoke.

But I should just say, that I'm serious, when I say . . . when I say that if you don't get the money—

ZACK: That you'll start throwing our furniture out the window, I got it.

ALIOUNE: Come on, no, / but—

ZACK: Hey, *own it*, you're a ruthless businessman, you gotta be makin' that paper, that's what you're about.

ALIOUNE: You have no reason to be angry at me.

ZACK: I'm kidding, dude, lighten up.

ALIOUNE: I don't think so. But okay.

(Abby enters, holding up two shirts.)

ABBY: Hey Alioune—Jesus!

(She opens the window.)

What were you guys, cutting a reggae album in here?

23

ZACK: I didn't want to open it because you get cold.

ABBY: Did you smoke more than one bowl?

ZACK: No!

ABBY: Because the last thing I need is you turning into a pot-head. Alioune, this one—

(She holds up a shirt.)

Or—

(She holds up the other. Alioune looks.)

ALIOUNE: Show me the first again—yes, that one. The other, I like it, but . . .

ABBY: It washes me out, right? It's so sad, I bought it in the sum-mer when I was all brown and healthy and now it makes me look like a vampire.

ALIOUNE: A little.

ABBY: Thank you, that was immensely helpful. When I ask Zack questions like that he just tries to figure out which one I like better and says that one.

ZACK: I have found it to be a fail-safe system.

ABBY: Hey, you're shivering. I'm not shivering, but you're shiv-ering.

(She closes the window.)

ALIOUNE: I should get back to the office.

ABBY: Oh—okay. Can I give you some cookies to take with you?

ALIOUNE: No, I— *(Off a look from Zack)* Yes! Yes, that would be wonderful.

ABBY: I'm just gonna get you a—

(She exits into the kitchen.)

ALIOUNE: *Alors, vendredi?*

ZACK: *Oui, j'ai bien compris.*

ALIOUNE: No matter what, I hope that we can still be friends—

(Abby reenters with a nice piece of Tupperware.)

ABBY: What happened, did you guys just break up?
ZACK: You're giving him our good Tupperware?
ABBY: It's the only clean one. He'll give it back.
ALIOUNE: I will, I will give it back.
ZACK *(Under his breath)*: I love that Tupperware.
ABBY: Here you go, please say hi to Amina. Oh God.
ALIOUNE: What?
ABBY: Do you ever just step outside yourself and see yourself?
　　I just saw myself handing over a Tupperware full of cook-
　　ies I baked saying, "please say hi to Amina."
ZACK: That is what just happened.
ABBY: It's okay. I can have all the trappings of a person I hate
　　and still be a person I like, right?
ALIOUNE: Thank you for the cookies. *(To Zack)* And the . . .

*(Zack salutes him, somewhat ironically. Alioune exits. Zack
is still shivering.)*

ABBY: What's wrong with you?
ZACK: I think I might have smoked a tad too much weed.

*(She goes to him and holds him. He burrows into her with
surprising urgency.)*

ABBY: Whoa. Hey, there. Hey.
ZACK: I'm sorry.
ABBY: That's okay, baby, I just took a valium.
ZACK: No, I mean, about . . . before.
ABBY: Oh.
　　No, that, that makes total sense, I just, I feel bad, that
　　I haven't / been satisfying you.
ZACK: No no no—
ABBY: Well, the proof is in the pudding, so.

ZACK: I don't want you to think that, it has nothing to / do with—

ABBY: We'll work on it, right? We'll work on it.

(Brief pause. They kiss, chastely, tenderly.)

What did Brigitte want?

ZACK: To remind me there's a staff meeting tomorrow morning.

ABBY: Did you need to be reminded?

ZACK: No.

ABBY: But I bet it was still nice to hear from her.

ZACK: Hey.

ABBY: She's really tall, isn't she? She's one of those really tall women who wears high heels anyway?

ZACK: She is not tall, and not a threat.

ABBY: Promise?

(Another sweet kiss.)

ZACK: Listen, do you want to get out of here?

ABBY: It's too early for dinner.

ZACK: No, I mean—get out of Paris.

ABBY: I thought if we leave we can't get back in.

ZACK: That's true.

ABBY: So . . . what are you asking me?

ZACK: What you want. What *you* want.

ABBY: You have a job here, Zack.

ZACK: I know.

ABBY: Like a really fucking important job that you care about a lot. That *I* care about a lot. That's why we uprooted ourselves and came here.

ZACK: Uh-huh.

ABBY: So . . .

ZACK: So, maybe that's not as important to me as you being happy.

ABBY: Aarrrrghghhhh!

ZACK: What?

ABBY: I am so tired of this fucking pressure to be happy. I am not happy, okay, that's just not my, like, mode of being, so if that's what you're trying to accomplish, *stop*. I'm pissed that you fucked up the visas and / we can't—

ZACK: It wasn't / me that—

ABBY: Or whoever, that whoever at Doctors Without Borders fucked up the visas and we can't see my family, and I'm upset that you came home from work early to jack off because you thought I'd be out, I'm not feeling great about those things, but just . . . live with it. Because I am so fucking proud of you, of what you're doing here, and I'm sorry I'm a pain in the ass sometimes, but I do not. Want. To leave. All right?

(Pause. Softening) Homey?

ZACK: Okay.

(She takes his face in her hands. They kiss. It deepens.)

ABBY: Is this okay?

ZACK *(While kissing)*: Mm-hm.

ABBY: What?

ZACK: Mmmmm.

(He pushes her down on the couch. She reaches to take off her shirt.)

Scene Two

Several hours later. It's dark outside. Abby and Zack sleep deeply, mostly naked and entangled.

   Silence, except for their breathing.

   A phone vibrates. They continue to sleep. Around the fifth time it vibrates, Abby lifts her head.

ABBY: Homey, I think that's—
ZACK: Shhhh. No it's not.

   (It has stopped. They drift off again. After several seconds it begins again.)

ABBY *(Drowsily)*: Baby, you gotta let me up.

   (He grunts.)

   It could be my dad.
ZACK: He'll call back.

ABBY: It could be about Meg.

(Reluctantly, he lets go of her and she clambers off him, brutally stubbing her toe on the way to the phone.)

Ouch! Fuck!
    Arrrgh!
ZACK *(Waking up from having drifted off again)*: Whatsa matter.

(She answers the phone.)

ABBY: Hello? Shit. Hello? Daddy? Yeah, hi. Sorry. I just stubbed my toe and it hurts like a motherfucker. No I'm fine, I'm okay. Fffffff. I'm okay. What's up?

(She hops over to sit as she listens.)

When?
    Oh my God.

(Zack sits up.)

Well of course I'm gonna—don't be ridiculous.
    Fine, but you can't ask me not to worry, that's just . . .
    What time?
    Will you call me when you know?
    Are *you* okay?
    That was unconvincing. Once more, with feeling.
    Yeah. Yeah.
    (Almost a whisper) Yeah.
    I'm here, anytime, okay? Whenever.
    Love you too.

(She hangs up.)

ZACK: What's up?
ABBY: They're gonna have to induce. I guess her blood pressure /
just . . .

ZACK: Oh, no.

ABBY: Dad says it's a totally standard procedure but he sounds like he's been crying. He gets this throaty thing in his voice.

ZACK: I've heard it.

ABBY: Oh, right. Of course you have.

ZACK: It is standard.

ABBY: Yeah?

ZACK: Really standard.

ABBY: Tell me more about that.

ZACK: Um, the chances of anything going wrong with either mother or baby in a major hospital in New Jersey are virtually zero.

ABBY: Thank you.

You did an OB rotation, right?

ZACK: Yup.

ABBY: So you know what you're talking about.

ZACK: Homey? They're gonna be fine. I mean I can't promise that child will be good *looking*, given the DNA in / question.

ABBY *(Laughing)*: God, what does she see in—?

He loves her. He really loves her. I bet he's being so great right now.

(Pause. She smiles bravely.)

ZACK: Now let's see that toe.

(She hops over to him and offers her foot.)

So which—*oh*. The swollen one, with the broken toenail?

ABBY: Oh, is it—?

ZACK: Homey, this is really impressive.

ABBY: Thank you. Do you think it's broken?

ZACK: I don't know, how does it feel when I do / that—

ABBY: Aa-aahhhhhhh! Ow! Ow!

ZACK: Sorry.

(He takes her toe in his mouth.)

ABBY: Ew! Is that—what they taught you in medical school?

ZACK *(With his mouth full)*: That's what they taught me in loooove school.

ABBY: That's so gross, I have a plantar's wart on that foot.

ZACK: Mmmmmmmmm.

ABBY: Zack!

(He takes her toe out of his mouth and kisses it. He stands.)

Where are you going?

ZACK: Ice.

(He exits into the kitchen. We can hear him opening the freezer, getting ice out of a tray, then assembling some kind of baggie. He reenters and applies the ice to her foot.)

ABBY: I like it when you doctor me.

ZACK: I'm gonna give you a *very* special rate.

ABBY: Ice is so *cold*.

ZACK: Upside? Much harder for you to run away from me now.

ABBY: Have you noticed that everything is starting to take longer to heal?

ZACK: Since . . . ?

ABBY: Since we're getting old. We are in physical decline.

ZACK: Will it affect your downward-facing dog?

ABBY: The physical decline? Definitely.

(She watches affectionately as he continues to doctor her.)

I'm still sad we had to leave Baltimore before your graduation.

ZACK: We had to be here.

ABBY: I know. But I wish I could've had that moment, to celebrate you.

ZACK: You celebrate me all the time.

ABBY *(Laughing)*: That is so not true. I complain all the time.

ZACK: In your complaints there is a perceptible undercurrent of celebration.

ABBY: Really? Good. I mean for there to be.
    What time is it?
ZACK: Almost eight.
ABBY: Jesus. How did we sleep so long?
ZACK: Drugs.
ABBY: Oh, right.
    (Remembering something else, suddenly) Right.
ZACK: What?
ABBY: Nothing.

(He checks the positioning of the ice pack and reapplies it.)

Did you read my sister's last email?
ZACK: Um . . .
ABBY: Her "third trimester report," or whatever?
ZACK: I have to admit, that *might* have gotten lost in my inbox.
ABBY: It's fine, you know I don't care, but she actually wrote
    about, um. Mom's death, and becoming a mom without
    having a mom. And it was very Meg, so it was all full of
    like . . .
ZACK: Clichés.
ABBY: Um, okay, that's actually not what I was going to / say.
ZACK: Sorry.
ABBY: No, yeah, I guess clichés, but just that writing style of
    hers where she's pretending to be very breezy and casual
    and unnecessarily abbreviating words and stuff but actu-
    ally dropping these / huge—
ZACK *(With emphasis)*: Oh God, totally.
ABBY: So, I'm allowed to say these things but you're not, okay?
ZACK: Yes. Silent.
ABBY: Anyway. On the one hand I found it kind of embarrass-
    ing, especially since she sends it to several hundred people,
    and on the other it was just very, um, honest. About her
    fears about parenthood, and how she expected to be done
    mourning by now, but especially with the hormones and
    everything she'll be driving, or doing laundry, or whatever,
    and she's suddenly caught out by these, like, waves of grief.

She said one of them lasted more than an hour, she had to cancel a meeting and sit at her desk and wait for it to pass.

I had never heard her talk about it like that before, she was the all-business one, you know?

ZACK: Yeah.

ABBY: So I've been meaning to write back to her about it but for some reason I haven't.

(Pause.)

ZACK: Yeah, that hormonal stuff, during pregnancy? That shit is no joke.

ABBY: Homey.

ZACK: What?

ABBY: That was not the point of that story.

(Brief pause.)

ZACK: I know.

(An ambulance is heard outside. As it approaches, it becomes very loud and casts red-and-white light inside the apartment. They wait for it to retreat.)

What would you write?

ABBY: Just that she's going to be an amazing mom. And that even though we're really different, I think she's made all the right choices. I really do think that.

ZACK: You wishing you had a corporate job and a husband who enjoys shopping for lawn furniture online?

ABBY: I'm wishing I felt less disdainful of everyone else and expected a little less from myself. So maybe if I were more like that I would have a corporate job and a husband who shops online, yes.

ZACK: I guess it doesn't occur to you that it hurts like hell when you say shit like that.

ABBY: It does occur to me, and then I say it anyway. I'm sorry.

(She moves the ice pack and gets up.)

All right. I'm gonna get ready for our D-A-T-E.

ZACK: You're feeling up to it?

ABBY: Oh, I'm tough. Say what you want about me; I am tough.

(She limps pathetically into the bedroom. He gets the pipe and attempts to smoke the dregs. It's no use. He burns himself and sucks on his finger. He goes to a drawer and opens it and sifts through it, but no luck.)

(Offstage) Fuck.

(In pain, she draws breath in through her teeth.)

ZACK: You okay?

ABBY *(Offstage)*: Yeah, just—getting these tight-ass jeans on. Jeggings. Do they call them jeggings, is that a thing?

ZACK: Maybe you should wear a skirt.

ABBY *(Offstage)*: Too late—I'm committed to it now. Ow. Fuck. Ow.

(After a few moments, she limps back out in tight, flattering jeans and her date shirt, brushing her hair. She looks great. He closes the drawer.)

What are you looking for?

ZACK: Uh, Advil. For you.

ABBY: We're out. From my epic migraine last week, remember? We can stop at Alioune's on the way down.

ZACK: Or we can go to the pharmacy.

ABBY: True, or we could just stop at Alioune's on the way—why are you looking at me like that?

ZACK: You look beautiful. You look really great.

ABBY: Thanks, but that's definitely not the face you were making.

ZACK: What face was I making?

ABBY: I would describe it as some combination of terror and burning hatred.

ZACK *(Edgy laugh)*: I have no idea what you're talking about. I like that shirt.

ABBY: You've seen me wear it before.

ZACK: Yeah, when, uh . . . when we had dinner with Charlie, right? Last spring?

ABBY: I've worn it a bunch of times.

ZACK: I think you wore it that night.

ABBY: I might've.

ZACK: I'm pretty sure.

ABBY: Okay . . .

I did ask you, earlier, about wearing this shirt—

ZACK: And I'm saying I like it.

ABBY: I think you're saying something a little more complicated than that.

ZACK: What do you think I'm saying?

ABBY *(Smiling)*: Zack? This is really childish.

ZACK: Why are you smiling?

ABBY: You're making me uncomfortable.

ZACK: All I'm saying. Is you look hot in that shirt.

(The subject seems to be uneasily dropped.)

And I'm very honored that you'd bust out your Charlie shirt for our D-A- / T-E.

ABBY *(Exiting, hobbling out)*: Okay! I am changing. My shirt.

ZACK: I'm not asking / you to change your shirt!

ABBY *(Offstage)*: I'll wear something that makes you feel more secure in your masculinity.

ZACK: I guess I hit a nerve, bringing up / Charlie.

ABBY *(Offstage)*: Fuck you!

(A long pause. Silence from the other room. Zack approaches the bedroom door and looks in.)

ZACK: Hey.

(Abby mumbles offstage.)

I'm sorry? Was that—human speech, or—?

(Abby mumbles offstage.)

I still can't / understand you.
ABBY *(Offstage)*: Doesn't matter.

(Pause. He lingers, now contrite.)

ZACK: Oh, now that—*that*, is fetching.

(Abby limps past him, not looking at him, in an oversized hoodie—probably his.)

ABBY: Ready!
ZACK: You think I'm gonna, what, be mad? That would be like me, to get upset that you're not dressed up enough?
ABBY: I was making an effort to inject a little romance, it was a stupid idea.
ZACK: Romance? Eeeww.
ABBY: Sorry, I'll never do it again.
ZACK: Hey.
ABBY: What?
ZACK: Hey.
ABBY: Stop saying "hey."
ZACK: I love you in that hoodie because I trust that hoodie to keep you warm. In your Charlie shirt / you would've—
ABBY: Stop calling it my Charlie shirt.
ZACK: You would've been cold.

(Pause.)

ABBY: I got a little dressed up when we saw Charlie because Charlie humiliated me when I was twenty-one and I will always feel like I have something to prove to him. I shouldn't have to explain that to you, because I'm entitled to some privacy and it has absolutely no bearing on our marriage.

(Brief pause.)

ZACK: Okay.

ABBY: And you shouldn't be so insecure. Or at least you shouldn't let me see it.

(Brief pause.)

ZACK: Okay.

(Long pause.)

ABBY: So where are we going?

(Blackout.)

Scene Three

The middle of the night. Zack enters with a sleeping Abby slung over his shoulder. He is out of breath. He brings her to the couch and drops her there. This wakes her up.

ABBY: Where am I?
ZACK: Home, homey.

(She laughs drunkenly.)

ABBY: Home homey home homey home.
     Did you know that— *(The rest of this sentence is muffled as she has rolled her mouth into a pillow)*
ZACK *(Taking off her shoes)*: Gonna have to repeat that.
ABBY: The word uncanny. It means unhomely. I mean, etymo-log-ic-ally. Or in German, or something. It's Freud. I'm dizzy.
ZACK: Your toe is turning some very exciting colors.
ABBY: Pretty ones?

ZACK: Mmmm. Yes. Very pretty. Not sure the toenail is long for this world, though.

ABBY: You might have to stay home tomorrow to take care of me.

ZACK: I might have to.

ABBY: Should we call Brigitte?

ZACK: Right now? No.

ABBY: I thought she might like to hear your voice.

ZACK: You're drunk and you're being silly.

ABBY: She never calls me back when I leave messages.

ZACK: *I* call you back.

ABBY: Also she doesn't pick up her phone. I think she screens me. I think she's threatened by American women.

ZACK: That's a good theory.

(He exits into the kitchen.)

ABBY: Where are you going?

(She lifts herself on an elbow but gets dizzy and drops back down.)

Did you think Amina was rude?

ZACK *(Offstage)*: What?

ABBY: Amina! I didn't want to say before because I thought you'd say I was— *(Hiccup)* paranoid because I was off my drugs. When we stopped for Advil. She was all weird and cold.

ZACK *(Offstage)*: I didn't notice.

ABBY: Maybe in France it's considered *(Hiccup)* rude to ask for Advil. We are strangers in a strange land.

(Zack reenters with a baguette and a large butcher knife and begins to cut slices of bread.)

Is that really the appropriate implement? For that little baguette?

ZACK: Everything else is in the sink.

(Abby sighs.)

ABBY: I'm a terrible housekeeper.

(He has cut a hunk of bread and hands it to her. She eats.)

You really didn't notice?

ZACK: What?

ABBY: Amina. I wasn't sure because you guys were speaking French but she seemed, like, icy.

ZACK: She was a little distracted, I guess. Another bite.

ABBY: I'm not that drunk.

ZACK: Okay.

ABBY: I'm not. And I'm not gonna puke again, I'm done.

ZACK: Hope so.

ABBY: Will you check my phone again?

ZACK: No one's called.

ABBY: Will you check?

(He gets her phone out of her bag.)

ZACK: Nope.

ABBY: Give it to me.

ZACK: You're not making any calls right now.

ABBY: I'm just gonna tell him I'm up. In case he's afraid to call.

ZACK: I doubt that, it wouldn't be the first time he called in the middle of the night.

ABBY: Hey, I don't like your tone.

ZACK: Take one more bite.

ABBY: He hasn't called in the middle of the night since the year after my mom died and it's not nice to bring that up.

ZACK: I'd like to have you to myself for one night, is that a lot to ask? Will you please take one more bite?

(She relents.)

ABBY *(Mouth full)*: You have me to yourself all the time.

(She bites and chews obediently.)

ZACK: You want some water?

(She nods. He exits to get it. She picks up the knife and looks at it with curiosity. He reenters with water.)

Whatcha doin' with that?

ABBY: Nothing.

ZACK: No playing with knives while you're drunk.

(Zach takes the knife from her and puts it down.)

Here you go. Just sip this, don't gulp or you'll get sick again.

ABBY: 'Kay.

ZACK: I'll be back in a couple minutes.

ABBY: Where are you going?

ZACK: Downstairs, I couldn't get the door closed while I was carrying you.

ABBY: I'm sure it's fine.

ZACK: Stay right there. Okay?

(Abby nods.)

Promise.

(Again. He exits. She waits a few moments. She gets up and limps to her phone. She dials. Zack reenters quietly.)

Hey.

(Abby gasps.)

What did I say?

ABBY: You were spying on me?

ZACK: I said no phone calls.

ABBY: But I just want my / dad to know—

ZACK: Abby? You're really drunk. You don't make smart decisions when you're drunk.

ABBY: I don't like it when you talk to me that way.

ZACK: Give me the phone.

ABBY: But then I won't hear it if he / calls.

ZACK: I'll hear it, and I'll answer it.

And I'll get you.

(He waits. She gives him the phone.)

You're gonna stay on the couch this time?

(She nods glumly and limps back to the couch. He waits until she is seated. He gives her a warning look and then exits again. Grumpy, she crosses her arms and sits back. She puts her feet clumsily up on the coffee table, sending a shock of pain through her toe. Woozily, she takes her foot in her hands and examines the toe. It looks bad. It may inspire a new wave of nausea. She steels herself and goes back to the toe. Part of the broken nail is hanging [of course we can't see that] and she decides to tear it off. She grabs hold of it and tries, but it's too painful. She gasps or cries out. She takes a few deep breaths. She remembers the large knife on the coffee table. She considers, picks it up, and returns to the task. With a determined but frightened little yell, she slices off the nail, and with it, some skin. It bleeds. A lot. She looks at the bloodied knife with some wonder.)

ABBY: Shit. Shit.

(She tries to stand, woozily falls back on the couch.)

Oh, no.

(She manages to stand, still carrying the knife. Her other hand covers her mouth. She limps woozily toward the bathroom. Offstage in the stairwell, we hear male voices in

French and footsteps racing up the stairs. Before Abby gets to the bathroom, Zack rushes in, pursued by Alioune in his boxers.)

ALIOUNE: *C'est quoi ce bordel?! Qu'est-ce que tu fais?*
ZACK: *Détends-toi, écoute-moi, c'était une méprise!*

(They see Abby with the bloody knife, wavering. She looks at them. She doubles over and vomits.)

Scene Four

About half an hour later.
 Zack is on his knees cleaning the floor. Alioune stands nearby.
Amina sits on the couch with a baby monitor.
 A long silence.

ZACK: You guys are very sweet. But you don't have to stay.

(Alioune and Amina look at each other. More silence.)

In college. This is just background for you guys. In college.
Abby got so drunk she lost like twelve hours of her life.
They say it's possible to be the kind of alcoholic who only
drinks once a year, but that once a year just gets dangerously
wasted? Abby's not a frequent drinker, she's actually a semi-
vegan, not sure if you guys knew that. So: twelve hours. She
"came to" or whatever in Bridgeport, which is—um, well
doesn't matter, but take my word for it she had no reason to
be there. And she was wearing clothes that she didn't own

as of the day before. Mental hygiene—that's the creepy name they had in college for, like, the psych part of the health center—they thought she might have had a severe break, like, schizophrenia or whatever. But nope. She was just drunk.

That was around the time her mom got sick.

Oh, Amina, je suis desolé, je viens de dire—

AMINA: I understand.

ZACK: Oh. We've always spoken French before.

AMINA: Because you needed to practice.

(Zack laughs, but she wasn't joking.)

ZACK *(Lightly)*: Guys, seriously, get out of here, I feel like an asshole, it's three in the / morning—

ALIOUNE: What were you doing in our apartment, man?

ZACK: Uhhhhhhh, right. Yes, I do owe you an apology about that.

That . . . was . . . totally my bad . . .

ALIOUNE: Please, no lies.

ZACK: I'm telling you, man, I was, it's embarrassing. I'm humiliated. I was looking for weed. I'm out. So.

AMINA: *C'est quoi?*

ALIOUNE: */ Rien.*

ZACK *(French accent)*: *Marijuana.*

(Alioune shoots Zack a frantic look.)

AMINA: *What?*

ALIOUNE: You know I do not do that.

ZACK *(Backtracking)*: No, I know, which was another reason it was so incredibly stupid.

AMINA *(Seeing through this)*: *Je vais te tuer. Et tu le garde à la maison? Avec les enfants?*

ALIOUNE: *C'est pas vrai!*

AMINA: *Oh, ouais . . .*

ZACK: No, he's—I'm—that was. Shit.

AMINA: Yes. Shit.

ALIOUNE: You have a problem. You think you deserve whatever you want, when you want it.

ZACK: No, I—

ALIOUNE: You think you can just take from others.

ZACK: I don't think that. I realize I have totally fucked up with you, with both of you, on a number of / counts—

AMINA: Yes, I think this is a fair, euh—

ZACK: Assessment, right, and you're furious at me, and I get that, but I swear to you that I have total respect for / you—

ALIOUNE: Ha!

ZACK: No, come on, man, I do, and I know I haven't deserved your patience, or your kindness—

AMINA: You could have hurt my children.

ZACK: I would never hurt your children.

AMINA: You come inside our home, it's the middle of the night, you are crazy.

ZACK: I would never, ever, in a million years hurt your children.

ALIOUNE: The problem, it's we don't know you. I thought I knew you.

ZACK: You do know me, let's not be melodramatic.

AMINA: Melodramatic? You break into our house to find drugs, we come upstairs, your wife is covered in blood, she has fallen in her, euh, her sick, you owe four months rent and you lied to us about where you work, sorry we are so melodramatic.

ALIOUNE: Okay, Amina.

AMINA: Okay what Amina, somebody has to say. The number you gave as a reference, at *Médecins Sans Frontières*, it does not exist, so what else have / you lied about?

ZACK: What number—what?

ALIOUNE: Don't pretend.

ZACK: Did I—make a mistake on one of the forms? I'll get you the right number, I'll get it / right now.

ALIOUNE: Bullshit.

AMINA: Maybe, maybe you made a mistake, but the point is, with everything else, we don't know. It can't work like this, where we can't trust you, so you have to go.

ZACK: I'm working on getting you all the money I owe. Alioune
    said I have until Friday.

ALIOUNE: Yes, by tomorrow you have to pay.

AMINA: And then you have to leave.

(Zack looks at Alioune in disbelief.)

Or maybe you would like to explain to the police why you
    broke into our apartment. If you prefer, we can call them in
    the morning. What do you think, Alioune?

ALIOUNE: If Zack prefers, we can call them right now.

AMINA: Okay. So you will let us know.

*(Through the monitor, we hear a baby fuss slightly—a few
cries, then he is quiet again.)*

ALIOUNE: *Tu veux déscendre?*

(Amina listens a few more beats.)

AMINA: *Non, il dort, ça va.*

*(Zack has finished cleaning the floor. He picks up the bloody
knife. Amina flinches.)*

ALIOUNE: Hey, what are you—

ZACK: I'm just gonna—whoa, I'm going to the kitchen. To
    clean it. Okay with you guys? Jesus, I'm behind on the rent,
    because you people fucking gouged me for this place, I'm
    not a psychopath.

(He exits. Alioune and Amina speak quietly.)

AMINA: *Qu'est-ce que tu penses?*

ALIOUNE: *Merde, je suis fatigué.*

AMINA: *Ouais, moi aussi, mais . . .*

ALIOUNE: *Allons-y, nous pouvons décider demain.*

AMINA: *Mais . . .*

ALIOUNE: *Quoi?*

AMINA: *Abigail. J'ai peur de la laisser avec lui.*

ALIOUNE: *Non non, il n'est pas dangereux. Il est stupide, il est menteur, mais il n'est pas dangereux.*

AMINA: *Tu es sur?*

ALIOUNE: *Il l'adore. Allons-y.*

(Zack reenters.)

ZACK: So . . . I was gonna go to bed. If I may have permission. Got a lot to do tomorrow.

ALIOUNE: Listen, I don't . . . I don't want to call the police—

ZACK: I hope you won't, man, I'm doing my best. And I really thought we were friends.

AMINA: Well that's what Alioune thinks, he think so too, you have no idea, he is so / upset—

ALIOUNE: *Amina, ça va.*

AMINA: You have embarrassed him, it is a shame.

(Amina exits. Alioune begins to follow.)

ZACK: Alioune. *(Alioune stops)* I'm sorry. We'll be gone tomorrow. We won't be a problem for you anymore. *(Alioune looks at him)* I need to talk to Abby. I need to . . . I need to talk to my wife.

(Alioune exits. Zack doesn't move for quite a few seconds. He goes into the bedroom, opening the door very quietly. After a few moments he emerges, closing the door softly behind him. He gets his coat and keys and leaves through the front door.

Several moments pass. Through the monitor—which Alioune and Amina have forgotten—we hear the baby begin to cry. The cries are relatively quiet and sparse at first, but soon it grows into full-blown wailing. Abby stumbles in from the bedroom, disoriented, ill. She can't place the sound of the infant crying.)

ABBY: Homey?

(On the monitor, we hear Amina's voice.)

AMINA *(Offstage, through the monitor)*: *Shhhhhhh, nous sommes là. Ça va, ça va, Maman est là.*

(The baby continues to wail.)

Scene Five

The next morning. Abby is lying on the couch with a pillow over her head. The sound of a key in the lock. Zack enters with coffee and pastries and a shopping bag.

ZACK: *Bon matin, chérie!*
ABBY *(Groggy, disoriented)*: Oh, God.
ZACK: Don't try to talk yet, drink this.

> *(He gives her the coffee. She drinks it. She squints up at him.)*

More.

> *(She obeys.)*

A little better?
ABBY: Not yet.
ZACK: You have not been so drunk since college, my little buddy.
ABBY: I fucked up.

ZACK: You feel nauseous?

ABBY: Yeah.

ZACK: You gonna puke again?

ABBY: I don't think s—did I puke?

ZACK: Twice. Once out, once here.

ABBY: Oh no.

ZACK: You don't remember?

(She shakes her head.)

So you don't remember . . . anything?

(She shakes her head again.)

ABBY: Oh wait. I remember a baby.

ZACK: A baby?

ABBY: I dreamed there was a baby here. I was confused, I thought it was my sister's. I thought my sister's baby had died and that way it made sense that it was in here screaming. Oh fuck!

ZACK: What?

ABBY: What time is it? Has she had the baby?

ZACK: I talked to your dad about an hour ago, he said her contractions were about five minutes apart, it's still gonna be a little while.

ABBY: I should call him.

ZACK: You should keep drinking that coffee until you're a little clearer in the old noggin.

ABBY: Did he say how Meg's doing?

ZACK: Her blood pressure's down a little, everything's looking good.

ABBY: Oh good. I'm so glad that wasn't her ghost baby.

ZACK: That must have been somebody else's ghost baby.

(Brief pause.)

ABBY: Did I dance on a table last night?

ZACK: You did.

ABBY: In that busted old hoodie?

ZACK: Yup.

ABBY: Classy.

ZACK: It was adorable. You had many admirers.

ABBY: Why did you let me drink so much?

ZACK: I tried to stop you. You were not happy about it.

ABBY: No?

ZACK: You said I was controlling and that your identity had been totally subsumed by me and that you don't know who you are anymore.

(Pause.)

ABBY: Yikes. Sorry.

ZACK: I tried not to take it personally.

ABBY: Good. That was super shitty, sorry.

(He smiles at her: "it hurts, but it's okay." He lifts a very small Christmas tree out of a shopping bag and places it on the table. Abby is delighted.)

Homey! Look what you did!

ZACK: You like it?

ABBY: Because we won't be at my family's, it's our first grown-up Christmas, with our own teeny tiny Christmas tree!

ZACK: I was raised to believe it's not the size of the tree that matters.

ABBY: It's perfect, it's the right size, for our first tree. It's a starter tree. When I feel better I'll go out and get little baby miniature ornaments.

ZACK: Now I'm actually starting to feel self-conscious about the size of / this tree.

ABBY: No, I love it. I *love* it. (*A warm moment*) We just have to find *very* small presents to put und—I'm kidding! I'm kidding! Oh, homey, I just got excited for Christmas.

ZACK: Good.

(He smiles, uneasily, but with a lot of love.)

ABBY: What time is it?

ZACK *(Getting the pastries out)*: Um . . . almost ten?

ABBY: Almost—why aren't you at work?

ZACK: Eat this.

ABBY: I can't eat that. I can't eat that there's chocolate in it I'm gonna yak get it away from me.

ZACK: O-*kay*.

ABBY: Don't you have a staff meeting?

ZACK: I couldn't leave you alone with your hangover.

ABBY: Did you call in sick?

ZACK: It's the holidays, everyone's taking it easy.

ABBY: Zack. Did you call Brigitte?

ZACK: Yes! I just, I wanted to spend the day with you. Okay?

(He kisses her.)

ABBY: Do I have puke breath?

ZACK: Little bit.

(He kisses her again.)

I love you.

ABBY: You too. Hey, you okay?

(A knock at the door. Zack puts a finger to his lips.)

What?

ZACK: Shh.

(He shakes his head.)

ABBY: Why are you—?

(There is another knock.)

Homey, I'm gonna get it.

ZACK: N-n-n-n-n-no.

AMINA *(Offstage)*: Excuse me, I hear you, can you please open the door?

(Abby breaks free of Zack's grasp and goes for the door.)

ABBY *(Having forgotten about her toe)*: Ow! Fuck.

(Another knock.)

I'm coming!

(She hobbles to the door. Zack stays where he is, frozen.)

Hi! Uh, *bonjour*, hi!

(Pause.)

AMINA: I just come for . . . I leave my, I don't know the English word. The . . . *l'interphone*?

ABBY: The . . . ?

AMINA *(With an exaggerated American accent)*: The interphone? The, euh, speaker, I can hear the baby.

ABBY: Oh . . . the *(Something dawns on her) Oh.* Oh oh oh oh oh. Hang on. Come in.

(She thinks, hard.)

I think . . .

(She limps off to the bathroom. Amina and Zack don't look at each other.)

(Offstage) Uh-oh.

(Abby reenters, bearing the baby monitor in several pieces.)

I'm so sorry. I remember taking it into the bathroom so that I wouldn't hear it, and then I could still hear it . . .

AMINA: I see.

ABBY: I was just trying to take the battery out, I didn't mean / to—

AMINA: Never mind.

(She begins to exit.)

ABBY: Amina—

(She stops.)

I'm so sorry. Of course we'll replace it.

(Something like a snort/laugh escapes Amina. Abby looks at Zack, who doesn't look at her.)

You know, the crying went on for a really long time.

AMINA: Yes, well, the baby is sick. He has a big fever.

ABBY: Oh no. Is he okay?

AMINA: No, I just tell you, he is sick.

(Pause.)

ABBY: I'm really sorry. I don't know what else to say.

(Amina exits.)

What the fuck was that?

ZACK: I don't know.

ABBY: She hates me, why does she / hate me?

ZACK: Nah, she's worried about the baby.

ABBY: I'm gonna feel horrible about that for so long. I'm gonna be like, what's that horrible feeling in the pit of my—oh, right, Amina *despises* me.

ZACK: She's just in a shitty mood.

ABBY: I'm sure there was an off button on that thing. I was so wasted, I guess I couldn't / find it.

ZACK: Hey.

ABBY: She's right, it's totally inexcusable behavior, I'm so embarrassed.

ZACK: She's the one who left it here, she should be apologizing to you.

(Pause.)

ABBY: She was here last night?

ZACK: Oh. You don't remember?

ABBY: No.

ZACK: They came up for a nightcap.

ABBY: We must've gotten home really late.

ZACK: Yeah, but they were up, because of the baby, so they came up for a drink.

ABBY: They left their sick baby downstairs and came up for a drink?

ZACK: No you're right, the baby wasn't sick yet, I'm not sure why they were up, but they heard us coming in . . . I was a little tipsy myself.

(Brief pause.)

ABBY: But they don't drink.

(Brief pause.)

ZACK: I was just using that expression, they didn't actually drink.

(Pause.)

ABBY: What's going on?

ZACK: What do you mean?

ABBY: I don't know, what do I mean?

(Pause.)

ZACK: I don't know.

(Long pause.)

ABBY: Homey? What's happening?

ZACK: I want to have a really good day with you today. Can we do that?

ABBY: I'm not sure.

ZACK: I need that from you, I need a few hours.

ABBY: And then what's gonna happen?

ZACK: Can we not talk about that yet?

ABBY: Really? You're really asking me that?

ZACK: Yeah.

ABBY: Uhhhhhh—

ZACK: Please.

ABBY: Oh, man. You look so scared.

(He tries to smile but the result is grotesque. Abby backs away from him. A long pause as it becomes increasingly impossible to deny what's about to happen. He takes a step toward her, she takes a step back.)

I'm gonna take a bath. I think I'd feel better if I took a bath, I'm so hungover I don't know what's what.

ZACK: Okay.

(She limps to the bathroom. She stops at the door.)

ABBY: Can I have my phone?

ZACK: You're gonna make phone calls from the bath?

ABBY: In case my dad calls.

ZACK: If he calls I'll bring it to you.

(Pause. Abby goes into the bathroom and closes the door. The water runs.

Zack takes a small bag of pot out of his pocket. He packs a bowl, opens the window, and smokes.

About a minute passes. The running water stops. Zack puts the pipe and pot away. He closes the window gingerly, as quietly as possible. He walks quietly to the bathroom door and listens.

Pause.)

You okay in there?

(He knocks gently.)

Abby? You okay?

ABBY *(Offstage, faintly)*: I'm fine.

(He lingers by the door.)

ZACK: Can I come in and look at that toe?

(She doesn't answer. He tries the door.)

Homey, you locked the door.

(Pause. He knocks again.)

Can you open the door for me?

ABBY *(Offstage, tearfully)*: I need a few minutes to myself.

(Pause.)

ZACK: I was walking around this morning, I was thinking about when you proposed to me.

 I was scared out of my mind, I was . . . twenty-two? I wasn't ready to get *married*.

 But I was also like, don't be an idiot, Zack, you're winning the lottery here, this is not gonna happen twice.

(Pause.)

Sometimes I worry that you wish I had said no, or said not yet, at least. Because I knew it was just because of your mom, and maybe you wanted me to be the mature one, to put on the brakes. Maybe if I was less selfish I would have done that.

(Pause.)

Is that what you think?

(Pause.)

Homey, now I'm getting really worried, can you please open the door? Or at least tell me you're okay?

(No sound from inside. He tries the door again. He jiggles it. He thrusts his shoulder against it.)

Fuck.

(He takes a few steps back and charges the door, which gives. He goes into the bathroom. He yells in alarm. The sound of frantic splashing and struggle goes on for several seconds, then Abby gasping.)

ABBY *(Offstage)*: No!

(The sound of slipping and falling. The sound of glass shattering. A loud "thunk.")

ZACK *(Offstage)*: Fuck!

(Zack enters carrying Abby, naked and dripping. They both have significant amounts of blood on them.)

Okay, baby. Okay, okay, baby.

(She is still catching her breath. He wraps her in blankets. He holds her.)

Shhhhhh. Shhhhhhhhh.
  You can't do that to me.
ABBY *(Shivering)*: I'm fine, I was just holding my breath underwater because I didn't want to hear what you were saying.

(Using whatever is handy, he attempts to clean the blood off both of them.)

ZACK: You're okay. It's a lot of blood, but these are just little cuts. Do you feel dizzy?
ABBY: No.
ZACK: You're okay.
ABBY: You're . . .
ZACK: What?
ABBY: You have . . .

(She points to a gash on his forehead. He touches his forehead, looks at his hand, and then goes into the bathroom. The sink runs, and then he emerges holding wadded-up toilet paper to his forehead. He goes back to her and holds her.)

ZACK: If this isn't the right time, then okay. But I want to have a serious talk about you going back on your meds.

(She tries to pull away from him, he pulls her in closer.)

You remember the last time you did something like this?
ABBY: I wasn't doing anything, I was just holding my breath.
ZACK: That's what you said right afterward the last time, you said it was an accident, you didn't count the pills right, and later you / admitted—
ABBY: This is different.
ZACK: Why did you lock the door?
  Huh?

ABBY: Because I'm afraid of you.

ZACK: Well, this is the other consequence of you not being on your meds, is paranoia.

ABBY: Don't make me feel like I'm crazy, Zack.

ZACK: Look at me. I love you. And I'm not gonna let anything happen to you.

ABBY: I want to talk to my father.

ZACK: Of course, of course you should talk to your father, but you should calm down a little first.

ABBY: I'm fine.

ZACK: You're—you're hungover, you're in withdrawal, I think your toe is infected and you're running a fever—

ABBY: Give me my phone. Give it to me. Please. Please. Please, give me my phone.

ZACK: Listen—

ABBY: I'll scream if you don't give it to me.

(Pause. Abby screams; Zack leaps onto her and covers her mouth, knocking over furniture on the way. They stay there for some time. The only sound is her breathing through her nose.)

ZACK: I'm not going to hurt you. You know that, right?

(Abby nods, terrified.)

Okay. Here's what's going on. We have to get out of here by tomorrow.

(She reacts by struggling, he subdues her.)

I got behind on rent. And I should have told you, and I'm sorry, but I didn't want to worry you, and I kept thinking I was gonna be able to catch up. And also I was ashamed.

(He tentatively lifts his hand off her mouth; she screams again and he covers her mouth.)

Please don't do that! I am trying to tell you the truth. We need to make some decisions, we need to make some plans. Which means we have to be on the same team, we have to be together on this. So can you promise me you won't do that again?

(After a moment she nods. He lifts his hand an inch away from her mouth and hesitates, then moves it away.)

Okay?

ABBY *(Practically spitting)*: Sure.

ZACK: Can you understand how that would have happened?

ABBY: Which part? *(Off his pained look)* I'm sorry, yes, I'm just supposed to say yes, right?

ZACK: No, I want you to be honest.

ABBY: No you don't.

ZACK: Yes I do.

(Brief pause.)

ABBY: Okay. You were right, I do wish you had said no when I proposed, that would have been better. I remember our wedding like I remember a nightmare. My mom was so sick she could barely stand for the ceremony, it was grotesque, I hate myself for putting her through that.

ZACK: You wanted her to see you get married before she died.

ABBY: That was idiotic and childish of me. And selfish. And loathsome. It was the most disgusting thing I've ever done, and I know it's not what she wanted for me, it probably helped kill her.

ZACK: That's a horrible thing to say.

ABBY: Why were you home yesterday?

Never mind, I don't want to know, I don't want to know.

ZACK: I think you do know.

(She sobs.)

Homey, it's okay, because we're in this together.

(Long pause.)

ABBY: Who's Brigitte?

Who was calling you when you said it was Brigitte?

(Another pause. He goes to his computer. He hits a few keys. He hits the volume key and we hear a Skype call initiating. Zack's phone begins to ring. She stares at him. Slowly, he takes out his phone and answers it. He speaks into the phone.)

ZACK *(His voice is doubled, a second behind, through the computer)*: I'm sorry.

(A long pause.)

ABBY: When did you lose your job?

(Pause.)

Did you ever have a job?

(Pause.)

I think I'm gonna—be sick again—
ZACK: Let me help you.
ABBY: Don't touch me!

(Pause.)

Why didn't we go to your graduation?
ZACK: Abby . . .
ABBY: You didn't graduate from med school.
ZACK: No.
ABBY: Did you *start* med school?
ZACK: Yes.
ABBY: Then *what happened*?
ZACK: I . . .

ABBY: What?

ZACK: I don't know. I finished my second year.

ABBY: And then?

ZACK: . . . I didn't do well on one my of exams, I was supposed
to retake it, and then I . . . missed a deadline to apply for
financial aid . . . I guess I didn't . . . fundamentally, it wasn't
what I wanted?

ABBY: Why didn't you just tell me?

ZACK: Uh, because you were suicidally depressed, and because
the fact that I was in med school seemed very important
not just to you but to your entire family.

ABBY: What are we doing here?

ZACK: You said you wanted to come to Paris.

ABBY: For a——?! For a *weekend*!

ZACK: I thought it was what you wanted.

ABBY: You should have asked me.

ZACK: I guess I felt like I did. Since I met you I have never done
anything without thinking of you first.

ABBY: That! Is the problem! Do you see that? Do you see how
completely impossible you have made it for me to love you
when you lack. Any. Actual. Core?

(A pause.)

ZACK *(Coldly)*: I think if you took a really good look. Abby.
You'd see that there are some things about you that are
pretty hard to love, but I figured out how to do it anyway.

*(Abby's phone vibrates. She is dying to answer it but doesn't
move. He takes the phone out of his pocket, silences it, and
puts it back in. A long pause. Abby speaks very carefully.)*

ABBY: Listen. I think something's really wrong with my toe,
I think I need to get it looked at.

(A pause.)

Zack. I'm serious, I need your help. Can you take me to the hospital?

(Longer pause. He looks at her uncomprehendingly.)

Homey. Please.

ZACK: I guess it was really stupid of me to think you might react with compassion.

(Brief pause.)

That was stupid, huh?

ABBY: . . . Zack—

ZACK: That's how I imagined it, but that was just . . . wow. So stupid.

(Pause. Abby is fighting panic.)

ABBY: I think . . . we're both really confused, and turned around—

ZACK: I don't think so, I think you've been pretty straightforward and clear.

ABBY: You have to understand, this is a lot for me to process all at once, I might have said some things that . . .

ZACK: Yeah?

ABBY: We both might have said some things we shouldn't have. And I'm sorry.

ZACK: The sad thing, homey, is that I don't trust you at all right now. I think you just want your phone and you want to get away from me.

ABBY: I do want my phone, and I need to get to a hospital, but I also . . .

ZACK: What?

ABBY: Understand why you—I'm mad at you, but I understand why you would've . . .

ZACK: You do?

ABBY: Yes. And I can be abusive. I can be emotionally abusive. I know that about myself, I have to work on that.

I'm sorry my first reaction was so selfish. You must have been so miserable. And you did that for me. I see that.

(She goes to him and kisses him, tentatively at first. He kisses her back passionately, almost violently. Their hands begin to run over one another's bodies. We can't see what is happening under the blanket, but suddenly there is a violent jolt and he grabs both her wrists. The phone is in one of her hands.)

ZACK: You gotta be fucking kidding me.

(He shakes her and the phone clatters to the ground.)

ABBY: I just want to talk to my father. I want to know if my sister's all right.

(He lets go of her. She falls to the ground.)

I won't tell them anything, I swear to God.

ZACK *(Quietly)*: I don't believe you.

ABBY: I promise, you can—you can sit next to me with a knife—

ZACK: I don't want to sit next to you with a knife, God, what do you / think I—

ABBY: I won't tell them, I won't tell them, just let me talk to them. And then take me home.

ZACK: That's what you want?

ABBY: Yes. We need to go home together and heal. We can get a tiny apartment and I'll work, it would be so good for me to work, I don't care, I'll do anything, and you can take some time to figure things out. That's what you didn't get, you didn't get any time. And I've had a lot.

ZACK: That's true.

ABBY: I can take care of you for a change, I think that would be so good for both of us.

ZACK: That sounds nice.

ABBY: Right?

ZACK: That sounds really nice.

ABBY: We just, we got off track, we lost our way, right? We can start over.

(He doesn't believe her, but it's nice to hear her talk like this. The phone on the floor vibrates. She doesn't make a move for it. She keeps her focus warmly on him. After it vibrates a few times, he picks it up and answers it.)

ZACK: Hello.
    Hi, Kevin. What's up?

(He looks at Abby, she looks back at him.)

Wow. That was fast. Not that I expect anything less from Meg.

(They keep looking at each other.)

That. Is . . . amazing.

(He is deeply moved. He smiles at Abby.)

That's terrific news.
    You know, it feels great. I've been many things before, but I've never been that.
    She's right here. She's so eager to talk to you. I'm gonna put her on.

(He gives her the phone. She takes it uncertainly.)

ABBY: I'm just gonna—

(She gestures toward the bedroom. He nods. She looks at him as she exits, answering.)

Hello?
    (Tearfully) Hi, Daddy, I'm so happy to hear your voice. How is she?

(She closes the door behind her. Her voice can be faintly heard through the bedroom door.

Zack stands still for a few moments, watching the door.

He goes to the window, opens it, and looks out at Belleville.

After several moments, he turns and walks to the kitchen.

He reenters, carrying the knife.

He goes to the bedroom door and listens for several seconds.

He gets one of the dining chairs and drags it quietly into the bathroom, closing the door behind him.

From within the bathroom, we hear him position the chair against the door.

We hear the water run for about twenty seconds and stop.

We hear Zack get into the bathtub.

Moments later, we hear the knife drop.

Some time passes.

Abby can still be heard within the bedroom.

The bedroom door opens and she enters, dressed, still holding her phone. She looks somehow cleansed and hopeful.)

I'm just gonna tell him.

Zack. They named her—

(She looks first to the open window, then to the closed bathroom door.)

Homey?

(She crosses to the bathroom and knocks.)

Homey? Zack?

(She tries the door. It's locked. She tries throwing her weight against it but it doesn't move. She backs away from the door, horrified, lucid.)

Daddy, I need your help. I need you to come get me.

(Lights out.)

Scene Six

Several days later. Amina and Alioune are cleaning in silence. They speak quietly, almost inaudibly, in French.

ALIOUNE: *Merde.*

> *(Pause.)*

AMINA: *Ouais. Incroyable.*

> *(Amina goes into the bathroom to retrieve something and comes back into the living room, leaving the bathroom door open.)*

> *Tu as le——?*

ALIOUNE: *Le quoi?*

AMINA: *Je le vois, il est là-bas.*

> *(Amina gets the broom from another part of the room. Several moments pass.)*

AMINA: *T'as quelle heure?*

ALIOUNE: *Euh ... un instant ... (He looks at his phone) Dix heures moins cinq.*

AMINA: *Oh. Il est encore tôt.*

> (*Long pause. They keep cleaning. Amina picks up the wedding album from the table. She looks through it for a few moments before hesitantly dropping it in one of the garbage bags.*
>
> *Amina gets a bucket from the bathroom. She returns to the living room and gets down on her hands and knees with the bucket, sponging a spot on the floor.*
>
> *Alioune stops his cleaning for a moment to watch her.*)

ALIOUNE: *Je suis désolé.*
Amina.

> (*She stops scrubbing.*)

Je suis désolé.

AMINA: *Oui, je t'ai bien entendu.*

> (*Pause.*)

Ça va. C'est pas une catastrophe.

ALIOUNE *(Laughing slightly)*: *Non?*

AMINA: *En fait, non.*

> (*She gives him a small, forgiving smile.*)

Allons-y. On a beaucoup de choses à faire.

> (*They return to their work. Very slowly, the lights fade.*)

END OF PLAY

Amy Herzog's plays include *After the Revolution* (Williamstown Theatre Festival, Playwrights Horizons, Lilly Award); *4000 Miles* (Lincoln Center Theater, Pulitzer Prize finalist, Obie Award for the Best New American Play); *The Great God Pan* (Playwrights Horizons) and *Belleville* (Yale Repertory Theatre, New York Theatre Workshop, finalist for the Susan Smith Blackburn Prize). She has received commissions from Yale Repertory Theatre, Steppenwolf Theatre Company and Playwrights Horizons. She is a recipient of the Whiting Writers' Award, the Benjamin H. Danks Award from the American Academy of Arts and Letters, the Helen Merrill Award, the Joan and Joseph F. Cullman Award for Extraordinary Creativity and the *New York Times* Outstanding Playwright Award. She is a Usual Suspect at New York Theatre Workshop, and an alumna of Youngblood at Ensemble Studio Theatre, Play Group at Ars Nova and the Soho Rep Writer/Director Lab. She has taught playwriting at Bryn Mawr and Yale. She received an MFA from the Yale School of Drama.